ISBN: 978-1-7374478-0-1

Note: he information shared in this book should be used for inspirational purposes and should not be used as a means of diagnosing or treating a mental health issue. It is recommended to seek the advice and services of a doctor or mental health provider as needed.

www.confidentlily.com

SHE Exudes

A CONFIDENCE AWAKENING DEVOTIONAL & JOURNAL

A. RENEE' ROBERTS

This devotional belongs to:

_____

Confidence, Faith, & Prosperity

"With confidence you have won before you have started. If you have no confidence in self, you are twice defeated in the race of life." - Marcus Garvey

Sis, are you ready for the shift? You are about to embark on a journey into learning more about who you are, who God has purposed you to be, and how you can defeat any self-conceived negative attitudes and outlooks. As I studied and wrote this journal, it increased my knowledge and gave me the boost of confidence that I needed to conquer negative thoughts and continue to push toward greater heights. I pray that it will do the same for you. Even strong women need to be refueled and reassured of the power that lives within. You're already equipped with the tools that you need to live your best life. The question is, *"Do you know how to use them?"* When you know how to use the tools that you already possess, you will begin to exude a confidence propelled by faith in God that leads to a life of prosperity.

Devotional contents include:

- 25 thought-provoking devotionals, scriptures, affirmations, and inspirational context.
- A section to journal your thoughts and prayers based on the devotion.
- A Personal Reflection section that can be used as space to document your goals, progress that you've made on those goals, or write additional prayers on each subject.
- A Confidence Builder Tool that can be used as an aid to visually see areas for improvement and to document attainable action plans.

Let us then approach God's throne of grace with confidence so that we may receive mercy and find grace to help us in our time of need (Hebrews 4:16, NIV).

Dedication

A recent study done by the Dove Self Esteem Project revealed that seven in ten girls believe they are not good enough or do not measure up in some way, including their looks, performance in school, and relationships with family and friends (Real Girls, Real Pressure: National Report on the State of Self Esteem, June 2008). Unless intervention occurs while the girl is still young, the chances are that she will continue to struggle with confidence issues into adulthood.

To the woman who currently feels or has ever felt like you weren't smart enough, capable enough, beautiful, loved, valued or anything in between, this book was written with you in mind. You are a queen and were created to do *Great Things*! At times we all need reminders of the power that lives within and nuggets of wisdom to help us continue to grow. With wisdom and power, we can *Exude Confidence, Faith, and Prosperity*!

To the woman who showed me that there were no limits to what a woman could do and instilled the Word of God in my life, this book is dedicated to you! Thank you, Mom, for the values and seeds of strength and tenacity you implanted in me throughout the years.

-A. Renee' Roberts

God has not given me the spirit of fear. I can and will be courageous!

THE ORDER OF STRENGTH AND COURAGE

"Have I not commanded you? Be strong and courageous. Do not be afraid; do not be discouraged, for the Lord your God will be with you wherever you go." - Joshua 1:9 NIV

With my mouth, I say, "I am strong!" I am not afraid! I am optimistic and determined! Yet, sometimes I don't feel that way. In fact, sometimes, my spirit feels so low that my physical being doesn't feel strong at all. My circumstances are so daunting that I am genuinely afraid to face them. Seeing the bright side of things seems so obtuse because it is dark and cloudy from my perspective.

When I leave my home, I perk up a bit, but when I am alone with my thoughts again, I feel insecure. Thoughts start to form in my mind, such as, you aren't strong enough to handle this. *Who do you think you are? Things are not going to work out for you. No one cares about you, and you're all alone.* If you've ever heard any of those thoughts or felt the opposite of the affirmation you've been trying to recite, I've got news for you...

It is the enemy that is trying to steal, kill, and destroy you!

Thoughts are attacked first, and then he will set his eyes on attacking your spirit. Once that is complete, he will escalate the unfavorable circumstances surrounding you in an effort to kill you physically. Why does he do this? It's simple. Payback! You are a child of the Most-High God, and that upsets him. He knows that through God and His son, Jesus, you are mighty and victorious! He doesn't want to see you succeed, overcome, and have power over him!

In Joshua 1, the Lord is reminding us with great assurance to be strong and courageous. He already knows the tricks of the enemy and that the road to victory won't be easy. He reminds us that we have somewhere to go, something to achieve, and that he will be with us every step of the way! We have to just continue with the order He has given us and not sway from righteousness. Doing so will lead to prosperity. Will you follow his order today?

JOURNAL: What negative self-talk have you experienced that may lower your self-esteem and prevent you from accomplishing your goals? What things have you been discouraged or afraid to do that would make you feel empowered? In what ways can you counter those negative thoughts and fears with something positive?

_____

_____

_____

_____

_____

_____

_____

_____

_____

_____

_____

_____

_____

_____

_____

_____

_____

_____

_____

_____

_____

PRAYER: Be open and real with God and share with Him every hurtful and negative thing that you've thought about yourself or that someone has told you. If you have begun to believe these falsities about yourself, pray that God removes those things from your perspective. Ask God to help mold you into the person that you want to become.

PERSONAL REFLECTION:

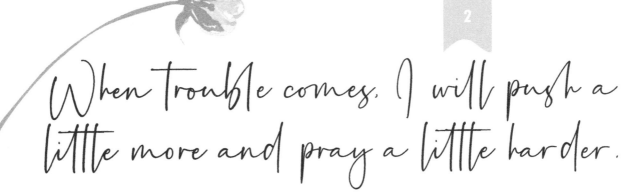

When trouble comes, I will push a little more and pray a little harder.

REASSURANCE IN TIMES OF TROUBLE

"I have told you these things, so that in me you may have peace. In this world you will have trouble. But take heart! I have overcome the world." - John 16:33 NIV

Some things are certain in life. One of them is that every being on this earth will, at some point, encounter trouble. We've all experienced it at some point and time. So why is it that when it comes, we often feel hopeless, confused, and worried? Why do we obsess over it and stress ourselves out? Trouble can be abrupt, scary, and unpleasant because we don't know exactly how things are going to work out, but as the gospel song says, *"Trouble don't last always!"*

Not only does trouble not last always, but the Lord has already given us His reassurance and remedy for dealing with it! He confirmed that there will be adversity and strife in this world, so there is no doubting that it will come, but He told us to "take heart!" That means to be courageous. Through Him, specifically His dying on the cross for us, He has given us peace, and He further reassured us that He has already conquered the world! The peace that He provides covers every ill feeling that you could ever have when experiencing trouble.

Furthermore, He gave us the remedy for dealing with it when it comes...be courageous! It takes courage to believe that our problem has already been worked out even when we can't see it. This is called having faith. Sometimes you will have to have audacious or, as some say, crazy faith to help see you through to the end.

As confident women, we must walk by faith and not by sight! The keywords in that last sentence are walk and faith. Don't just sit around waiting, wishing, and hoping that the problem goes away. You also can't ignore it. Ignoring it will not make it go away. Ask God to direct your paths on how you should proceed, move forward, and reclaim your peace!

JOURNAL: What trouble have you experienced recently that you could've handled better? In what ways could you have given your trouble to God in an effort to walk in peace? Were you fearful and worried about the outcome, or were you confident in God resolving it for you?

....
....
....
....
....
....
....
....
....
....
....
....
....
....
....
....
....
....
....
....
....
....
....
....
....
....

PRAYER: What trouble or problems do you still need to hand over to God? Ask the Lord to take your burdens and provide you with better tools to handle trouble in the future.

PERSONAL REFLECTION:

Even when I feel weak, through Christ, I am strong. I can get through this!

WEAPONS FORMED AGAINST ME WILL NOT PROSPER

"No weapon forged against you will prevail, and you will refute every tongue that accuses you. This is the heritage of the servants of the Lord, and this is their vindication from me," declares the Lord."
- Isaiah 54:17 NIV

It is difficult enough to wake up every day, embark on your journey, and counter every negative thought that comes to your mind to tell you that you are not enough or that the effort that you are giving is not enough. Daily self-talks are often very necessary to refute negative thoughts that want to inundate your mind.

The journey is even more challenging when faced with outside attacks, and you find yourself in an army of one, fighting a battle for your sanity and livelihood -- trying to defend yourself from being overtaken by the opposition. Their weapons of mass destruction against you are intimidating, hurtful, and seem to be in abundance. Every time you look around, there seems to be something else coming for you. With each blow, you begin to feel weaker and weaker. The little confidence you may have had in your abilities to win is now fleeting, and you feel like falling to the ground and waving your flag.

But... Hold On, Sis! Do Not Give Up! Do Not Be Dismayed!

The Lord has promised us that NO WEAPON forged against us will prevail! Looking on the outside, one might think that we are powerless or that we can be easily defeated. Ha! I'm so glad that Christ has given us the last laugh! Regardless of what is said about us, we will still stand. Regardless of how scary the enemy looks, we will not be afraid. Why? Because we are descendants of the Most High and Mighty, and we know that "vengeance is mine," said the Lord.

Stand firm and know that "You Got This!" You're a conqueror, and with the help of Christ, you can be victorious day after day. Your enemies may continue to try and stop your progress, but in this, we hope that their weapons will bounce off you like rubber, and the ditches that they dig for you will be the ditches that they fall in!

JOURNAL: What battles have you been fighting? Recall any victories, even if they are small. What area do you feel that you need strength in?

_____

_____

_____

_____

_____

_____

_____

_____

_____

_____

_____

_____

_____

_____

_____

_____

_____

_____

_____

_____

_____

PRAYER: In the areas you feel less confident in, ask God to strengthen and equip you with the necessary tools to win the battle. Pray that you will recognize the attacks of the enemy when they come and will be able to overcome them quickly.

PERSONAL REFLECTION:

It is okay to cry because I know that God will dry all my tears and answer my prayers in due time.

HOPE IN MOURNING

"He will wipe every tear from their eyes. There will be no more death or mourning or crying or pain, for the old order of things has passed away." - Revelation 21:4 NIV

The loss of a friend or loved one can be devastating to the heart, especially when unexpected. One would find themselves in mourning and questioning why God allowed it to happen. We know that there will be new life entering the world every day and other lives exiting the world. That is the way life goes; however, it doesn't negate the feelings of sadness, confusion, anger, loneliness, and despair that we may feel.

No man knows the day or the hour when they will leave this earth. That is why it is so important to show love, reconcile with Christ, and live life to the fullest. We may not understand why our loved ones had to leave, why some people experience suffering more than others, or why tragedies occur. However, we should never forget that God's will is best and that He will be there to comfort those who need to be comforted. He promised never to leave or forsake you; therefore, you can trust Him to get you through this season of pain. He can turn grief into joy and confusion into understanding.

"God didn't promise days without pain, laughter without sorrow, nor sun without rain, but He did promise; strength for the day, comfort for the tears and light for the way." - Unknown.

It's okay to cry. It's okay to mourn our loved ones and miss life as it once was but remain confident that you have the strength to continue on. When we are weak, He is strong. In times of darkness, He will bring light. You are still standing for a reason. You can make it through this time. Instead of mourning the past, begin to be thankful for the time that you had and know that there is still hope for better days to come.

JOURNAL: Are you in a period of mourning? What sadness and feelings of grief do you need to give over to God?

PRAYER: Pray about what you are experiencing in this time of sadness and ask God for the path and the strength to make it through. Ask God to help you feel worthy enough to move on with your life.

PERSONAL REFLECTION:

I am perfectly imperfect and flawlessly flawed! He has made me great!

LIVING WITHOUT ARROGANCE OR BOASTFULNESS

"For it is by grace you have been saved, through faith—and this is not from yourselves, it is the gift of God— 9 not by works, so that no one can boast. 10 For we are God's handiwork, created in Christ Jesus to do good works, which God prepared in advance for us to do." - Ephesians 2:8-10 NIV

Sometimes confidence can be mistaken for arrogance. Arrogance often starts with one feeling secure or assured in their abilities but then quickly graduates into an overwhelming sense of importance in one's abilities. There is nothing wrong with having pride. You've likely earned the right to be proud and happy about your accomplishments. However, when pride becomes self-absorbed and superior to others, it takes a negative turn. Confident women of God are never arrogant.

Confident women often have much to be proud of. Think about it. The act of getting to the point where you are happy, at peace, secure in who you are, and leading a prosperous life is no small feat! As women of God, we are entitled to live in the favor of God and enjoy His blessings. His favor is something to be excited about and shared with others as a testimony of how great He is. We are also encouraged to speak good things into existence and expect greatness because our father is rich. However, when we "forget" where our blessings come from and begin to boast about our gifts, we cross into another territory and are in jeopardy of having our favor taken away.

We should always remain humble and remember, as Ephesians says, that we are God's handiwork, created to do good works. Because of His grace, we are saved. Because He is faithful to His promises, we can attain the lifestyle that He stated that we were entitled to. Don't fall into the trap of thinking that you alone allowed you to get to where you are in life. Remember that you can do ALL things through Christ who strengthens you, but not ALONE.

JOURNAL: What are the accomplishments that you are most proud of? How did God help you to achieve those? Are there any areas where you feel that you could be more humble?

_____
_____
_____
_____
_____
_____
_____
_____
_____
_____
_____
_____
_____
_____
_____
_____
_____
_____
_____
_____
_____
_____
_____
_____
_____
_____

PRAYER: As you reflect on your gifts and blessings, begin to thank God for His awesome favor and pray that you will be a shining light and an example of God's mercy.

PERSONAL REFLECTION:

A dream deferred is not a dream denied. I will never give up on my dreams.

NEVER GIVE UP ON YOUR GOAL

"Not that I have already obtained all this, or have already arrived at my goal, but I press on to take hold of that for which Christ Jesus took hold of me. 13 Brothers and sisters, I do not consider myself yet to have taken hold of it. But one thing I do: Forgetting what is behind and straining toward what is ahead, 14 I press on toward the goal to win the prize for which God has called me heavenward in Christ Jesus."
- Philippians 3:12-14 NIV

Have you gotten complacent with where you are currently, and life has become a little too routine or dull? You may have climbed various levels to reach a certain level of achievement but then just became stagnant at the top. Have you plateaued in your current plan and neglected to accelerate your goals because you've gotten too comfortable on auto-cruise? At certain times in life, it is important to remain still, to grow in knowledge, and to wait for God to direct you to your next area of opportunity; but there are other times when we need to give ourselves a kick in the butt to get up and push for greater.

"A comfort zone is a beautiful place, but nothing ever grows from there."- Unknown

In Philippians, we find that Paul, having gone through all that he had, still did not feel that he had met his goal. He thought that there was more that God had called him to do. Paul felt that there was still a prize to be won and that he should push for it. He did not become comfortable with settling, but instead, he decided to act upon the feelings of greater that he possessed.

When God places a call upon your life, it often cannot be ignored. What is the dream that you once had that you have given up on? What goals did you give up on because outsiders and negative self-talk told you that it was not practical? What talents do you have that you are not utilizing?

Whatever it is, Sis, you have to press on to achieve those dreams and goals. If it is meant for you to do, it must be done! Forget about past attempts that may have failed. Believe that there are no failures, only lessons to be applied in future attempts. No great woman has ever achieved success by just staying at the status quo. Cast down all fears and slowness and pursue your dreams. You only have one life to live, and God has given you the authority to make it a great one!

JOURNAL: What hopes and dreams did you have when you were young? Are they still realistic and attainable today? Is there a goal that you would like to pursue, but you are afraid of doing so? If you are comfortable in your current state, what can you change to bring a little variety into your life?

PRAYER: As you reflect on your hopes, dreams, and goals, make sure to ask God to give you clear insight into which ones you should pursue and when. Pray that you will have the strength to reject fear as it comes and the endurance to achieve your goal.

PERSONAL REFLECTION:

I will choose a Queendom Mindset even when I don't feel like one.

CHOOSING PEACE OVER ANXIETY

"Do not be anxious about anything, but in every situation, by prayer and petition, with thanksgiving, present your requests to God. 7 And the peace of God, which transcends all understanding, will guard your hearts and your minds in Christ Jesus. Finally, brothers and sisters, whatever is true, whatever is noble, whatever is right, whatever is pure, whatever is lovely, whatever is admirable—if anything is excellent or praiseworthy— think about such things." - Philippians 4:6-8 NIV

Chances are that you or someone that you know has experienced feelings of deep fear and dread, excessive worrying, nervousness, persistent concern, or invalided panicking at some point. Those are all signs of anxiety and could become a disorder if it happens frequently. Did you know that anxiety disorders are one of the most common mental illnesses in the U.S. and are also most common in women?

Why women? One reason is that we have more hormone fluctuation than men. Another reason is that women tend to be more prone to stress than men. More stress can lead to more anxiety. The more stressful situations one has to deal with, the more limited their ability to cope with and subdue ill emotions effectively. As women, we have to protect our minds at all times.

As mentioned in Philippians, we should not be anxious about anything. Instead, we should pray, give thanks for our current blessings, and petition our concerns and requests to God. Now I know that this practice may be a little more challenging than it seems. Why is it so complicated, though? Christ has conquered every situation and even died to save our souls. There should be nothing that we should worry about, right? However, the enemy knows just how to pile on a little more stress here, add a little more heartache here, sprinkle a little drama in here, and before we know it... we've got ourselves a whole anxiety pie! The scripture tells us that God's peace will rise above ALL understanding regardless of what the situation looks like and that it will guard our hearts and minds. So, the key to defeating the enemy's recipe for disaster is to choose peace and to give our anxieties to God.

We must remind ourselves daily of all of the blessings that we've received throughout our lives. If it's hard to recall personal good things, think about the beauty of sunshine, the beautiful melodies of birds chirping, your favorite scent blowing in the wind, and any other wonderful thing that God has created. Doing so will recenter your peace and distract you from focusing on the negative.

Sis, I realize that doing this work on your own may take practice in addition to prayer. I recommend that you also seek wise counsel from a mental health professional to provide you with even more coping tools. The more tools you have in your tool belt, the better equipped you will be.

JOURNAL: Are there things in your life that you are worried or concerned about? How do you deal with stress and feelings of being overwhelmed?

PRAYER: Pray about the things that you need to have peace about. Cast your worries, cares, and doubts unto God. Pray that God sends you the right tools to manage your stress and anxieties.

PERSONAL REFLECTION:

My past does not define me. I am working today to improve my future.

NEVER FORGET THAT YOU ARE FORGIVEN!

"If we confess our sins, he is faithful and just and will forgive us our sins and purify us from all unrighteousness." - 1 John 1:9 NIV

We all have something that we've done that we are not proud of. Part of growing up and maturing is learning from your mistakes. Everyone has a past and thank God our past is not our present. We can also rest assured that our future is not exclusively reliant on what we've done in the past. The first step to receiving God's best is to acknowledge and confess our sins. When we repent from our wrongdoings, God forgives us immediately. He is not like a man in which you constantly wonder if you have truly been forgiven. He is loving and merciful.

Some women lack the confidence to be great because they have not forgiven themselves for things that have happened in the past. Often, they feel unworthy or unloved because someone told them that they could never change or placed a label on them. In the end, the only label that truly matters is that you are a child of God. Despite who your natural parents are or the walk of life you have come from, you are royalty! You come from a royal priesthood, and you are entitled to greatness.

Although we are striving to become exceptional women, we are not perfect. There may be times when we must ask for forgiveness again, and that is okay. Just remember who you really are, and that God has the power to forgive and blot out your sins. You are not broken beyond repair, and you are worth being saved! You can restart with a clean slate today.

JOURNAL: Reflect on anything that you need to repent and ask for forgiveness for. Is there anything that you have not forgiven yourself for?

PRAYER: In addition to asking for forgiveness, ask God to help you truly learn from your mistakes so that you do not repeat the same ones in the future.

PERSONAL REFLECTION:

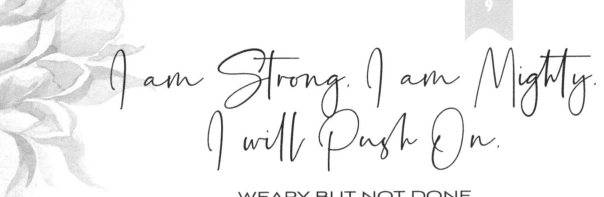

I am Strong, I am Mighty, I will Push On.

WEARY BUT NOT DONE

"Cause me to understand the way of your precepts, that I may meditate on your wonderful deeds. My soul is weary with sorrow; strengthen me according to your word." - Psalm 119:27-28 NIV

"I'm so tired" is a statement that I have often made. In fact, it is a statement that many multi-faceted women have made. Being weary, though, adds another degree of exertion. To be weary means to be worn out, drained, and exhausted. Let's imagine being weary with sorrow. I am visualizing a person walking through a desert tired, thirsty, sad, and dragging their feet through the sand. The person looks as if they are going to give up, but they keep trudging along. While visualizing this, I can identify with this person's perceived sadness. Deep down in my chest, I can feel the pit of hopelessness, and I can feel my face becoming stoic. Why? Because I know what it is like for your soul to feel weary due to disappointment, misfortunes, etc.

We will experience a degree of sorrow at some point in our lives. Each blow that we are dealt can make us weaker and weaker to a point where we, too, are just trudging along in life. Thankfully, we have access to an everlasting strength that is so much more powerful than we are! When my soul feels weary, and I begin festering on all of my problems and letdowns, I can just cry out to the Lord for strength, and He will provide.

The Book of Psalms says, "Strengthen me according to your word." This means that it has already been promised to us that He will be our strength when we are weak. "Cause me to understand the way of your precepts" indicates that we need to desire to understand God's law and His tenets. By doing so, we will understand more about our purpose and how we should abide in Him. When your mind is focusing on all of the negativity around you, that is the best time to meditate and redirect your mind on God's wonderful deeds. Remind yourself daily of the grace that He has given us and all of His miraculous ways. By doing so, feelings of sorrow can be redirected, and your strength can be renewed. Remember, weary does not mean that you're done.

38

JOURNAL: Reflect on times when you've experienced some type of sorrow. How do you know when you are at the point of becoming weary? What can you do to rest and renew? What are some wonderful works that you have witnessed God perform?

_____

_____

_____

_____

_____

_____

_____

_____

_____

_____

_____

_____

_____

_____

_____

_____

_____

_____

_____

_____

_____

_____

_____

_____

_____

PRAYER: Consider the areas in your life where you need God's strength and ask God for a renewal and refreshing of your mind, body, and spirit. Actively seek opportunities for self-care and personal meditation time with God.

PERSONAL REFLECTION:

10

I am uniquely and beautifully made. There is no one else quite like me.

IDENTITY CRISIS AVERTED

"For you created my inmost being; you knit me together in my mother's womb. I praise you because I am fearfully and wonderfully made; your works are wonderful; I know that full well." - Psalm 139:13-14 NIV

Who am I really? What do I enjoy doing? What is my purpose in life? Have I achieved the goals that I set for myself? Life can come at you fast, and before you know it, answering these questions may be a little more difficult to do than in the past. Time and life's experiences can change things and cause you to lose sight of your dreams and who you truly are.

Have you ever started or ended a relationship or a marriage, became a new mother, began or lost a job, lost a loved one, or gone through a traumatic event? If so, you know how easy it is to look at yourself in the mirror and not recognize the person you have become. Any of those stressful changes can shift your focus and perspective and cause you to doubt yourself. You may have even given up on a passion because that thing that you went through zapped all of your power, and you are just unsure if you can do it anymore. Additionally, outsiders may have been a negative influence by voicing their opinions about you which caused you to devalue your worth and abilities.

A confident woman knows who she is, what she wants, and what she is capable of. When our vision for ourselves is unclear, and we might be having a slight identity crisis, it is important to remember who our creator is. We are fearfully and wonderfully made. Don't let others dictate to you who you are or what your purpose is. God has a special plan for you that is perfect. Even if you have yet to discover what that plan is, know that something uniquely special makes you important in this world. When you start to question your worth, or whether or not you are qualified to do something, begin to pray, and thank God for equipping you with everything that you need.

JOURNAL: Reflect on the goals and expectations that you had for your life in previous years. Were any of those goals accomplished? In what ways have your expectations or focus changed? In what ways have your hobbies, likes, or desires changed?

PRAYER: In prayer, ask God to reveal and clarify your purpose in life. Pray for the ability to remain confident in who God has created you to be and to find peace in your unique identity.

PERSONAL REFLECTION:

11

I have self-control to tame my tongue. Anger will not overtake me.

SPEAK LIFE NOT STRIFE

"The lips of fools bring them strife, and their mouths invite a beating. The mouths of fools are their undoing, and their lips are a snare to their very lives." - Proverbs 18:6-7 NIV

"The tongue has the power of life and death, and those who love it will eat its fruit." - Proverbs 18:21 NIV

The ability to control our tongues and the words we utter out of our mouths is truly a great skill. Have you ever said something that you wish you could take back? Maybe it was something hurtful or rude to another person.

Perhaps you helped spread a rumor that you weren't quite sure of the accuracy of or told something that was spoken to you in confidence. Maybe you are so used to hearing others talk to you in a foul manner that it has become innate for you to speak to your family, friends, and others in the same way.

Could it be that you get a sense of pleasure when you are quick to "pop-off" or "set someone straight?" We know that hurt people hurt people. If your tongue is being used as a weapon of fire, just imagine the depths of that fire in the innermost places like your heart.

When people speak too quickly, they don't take time to think about what they're saying and how another person may interpret it. What you think are just words actually have the power to crush spirits, negatively affect someone's livelihood, and ultimately bring you a life of strife. Be quick to hear and slow to speak. Our goal should be to uplift and encourage our sisters instead of belittling them. Lying and backbiting is also not something that confident women participate in because they are aware that the fruit of their labors could be cursed.

When dealing with disrespect from men, don't make a mockery of yourself. Instead, maintain your dignity and self-respect and let God handle any wrongdoings. Most importantly, confident women speak life upon themselves.

They don't refer to themselves as mere objects or animals, nor project unbecoming things about themselves into the atmosphere. Why? Because once a thing is spoken, you can start believing it, and it has the power to manifest. Speak life, not death. Speak hope and not hopelessness. Let your tongue perpetuate good and not evil.

JOURNAL: In what ways have you used your tongue to manifest negatively or speak inappropriately to someone? What could you have done differently?

....
....
....
....
....
....
....
....
....
....
....
....
....
....
....
....
....
....
....
....
....
....

PRAYER: Pray that even in difficult situations that the Lord will bridle your tongue and give you the right words to say to others. If you have had thoughts or intentions of causing hurt, pray for a change and that you will be a vessel for speaking life instead of strife.

PERSONAL REFLECTION:

12

Christ can do all things but fail. He is working on my behalf.

FAITH AND THE RECIPE FOR SUCCESS

"Now faith is confidence in what we hope for and assurance about what we do not see." - Hebrews 11:1 NIV

If you are a creative person, you may often start a new project or task and have an idea of how you want it to look, but you don't actually know how it will turn out. Because you've worked with particular materials and tools before, you are pretty confident that your project will yield certain results. As you are working, you may have some doubts, but they are not severe enough to make you want to pull out of the task altogether, so you push forward. You stop to review your progress and realize that it is not quite coming out the way you were hoping it would, so you make a slight change. With some persistence, you have completed the project, and to your surprise, the finished product has exceeded your expectations!

That simple analogy explains how faith works. Faith is a belief or trust in something. In the King James Version of the Bible, faith is described as "the substance of things hoped for and the evidence of things unseen" *(Hebrews 11:1, KJV)*. I love this version of the definition because it magnifies the importance of faith. The substance of things hoped for indicates that it is an element or a critical part of hope. There is no hope without faith. When we hope for something, we wish, anticipate, or aim for something specific to happen. The evidence of things unseen means that we believe and are assured of something that we cannot physically see just yet.

This is the kind of faith that we have to have to overcome hurdles and change the trajectory of our lives. If you are praying that God restores or helps you to develop confidence, you will need to have faith to know that it is already done. You will have to believe that it is possible and see yourself as being a confident woman. This same principle can be applied to anything that we are pursuing or hoping for.

There is one caveat to the faith principle. We must also work our faith. Meaning that we can't just sit back and wait for something spectacular to happen... we have to put in some action.

According to the Bible, "faith without works is dead" *(James 2:20, KJV)*. Even though God is merciful and just, he is not our genie. He expects us to put in some action with our faith. Action combined with prayer and true faith is the recipe for success.

JOURNAL: In what ways have you practiced true faith recently? Are there areas where your faith needs to be restored? When doubt begins to creep in, what affirmations can you use to increase your faith?

....
....
....
....
....
....
....
....
....
....
....
....
....
....
....
....
....
....
....
....
....
....

PRAYER: Pray that God will increase your faith as you wait for what you hope will come to pass. Even when the outlook is not looking positive, continue to pray, for even a mustard seed of faith shows that you still believe that it can come to pass.

PERSONAL REFLECTION:

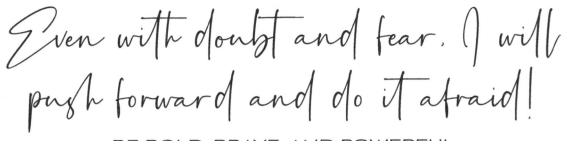

13

Even with doubt and fear, I will push forward and do it afraid!

BE BOLD, BRAVE, AND POWERFUL

"For the Spirit God gave us does not make us timid, but gives us power, love, and self-discipline."
- II Timothy 1:7 NIV

Have you ever struggled with imposter syndrome or letting your voice be heard? Do you find it difficult to assert yourself and claim your seat in places where you might be less familiar? Do you find yourself shrinking back when you are working to achieve an important goal or milestone? If you answered yes to any of those questions, you might need to be reminded that God has not given us a spirit of fear and that you have access to a divine power that is far greater than anything that we could ever conceive.

Confident women, regardless of their physical size, are strong and mighty. They are secure in who they are and their abilities. This doesn't mean that they won't face opposition from time to time that causes them to doubt themselves or be afraid. It means that when those thoughts come, they can quickly refute the opposing narratives. They continually remind themselves of scriptures like II Timothy 1:7, reset their mind, and renew their strength.

Some people are naturally shy and timid until they realize just how important and capable they are. In my youth, I was actually very quiet and shy. Why? Partly because I didn't feel that I had much to say or was afraid of what others would think of me. Going to college and meeting people from diverse backgrounds showed me that while we may all be different, we are very similar, too. Obtaining an education and working on my personal development caused me to become more appreciative of who I was and what I had to offer the world. Eventually, the shyness began to go away as I gained more confidence.

What happens when you have acknowledged your strengths and abilities but are going through a season of disappointment that has left you feeling powerless? This is when your discipline and use of sound judgment comes in.

Know that when you are weak and begin to believe the enemy's lies, that you need to draw closer to Christ. Submit to Him and allow His will for you to be made clear. Ask for direction and learn how to proceed with power. We cannot do it alone, but with the help of our Savior, we can be a mighty force to be reckoned with. Others will be amazed by our boldness and tenacity while we hang tight to our secret weapon, Christ Jesus.

JOURNAL: What are some examples of times when you have been bold and stood up for yourself? In what ways is fear holding you back? Are there any areas in your life in which you want to feel more empowered?

....
....
....
....
....
....
....
....
....
....
....
....
....
....
....
....
....
....
....
....
....
....

PRAYER: After reviewing your strengths and weaknesses, have an honest conversation with God on how you would like to improve. Seek Him for boldness and the power to reach the heights that you'd like to attain in life.

PERSONAL REFLECTION:

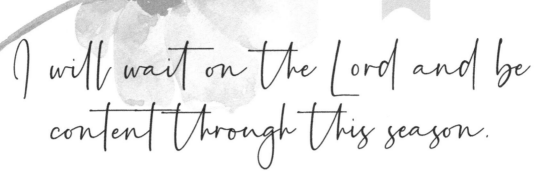

14

I will wait on the Lord and be content through this season.

THE HOPE THAT RENEWS STRENGTH

"but those who hope in the Lord will renew their strength. They will soar on wings like eagles; they will run and not grow weary, they will walk and not be faint." - Isaiah 40:31 NIV

What do you do when you have lost the ability to hope or when your strength begins to dwindle? To have hope is to have an expectation or desire for something to happen. It is a feeling of trust that what you seek will come to pass. If you have come to a place in life where you have grown tired and weary from the obstacles of life, don't give up! The path that you are currently taking may be rocky and filled with bumps along the way, but the power of Christ can give you the strength and willpower you need to walk upright even when you feel weak. You must continue to have faith and hope, even if only the size of a mustard seed, to know that you can still be victorious!

As women, we hold a kind of strength and perseverance that is uncanny, but that doesn't mean that we do not get down from time to time. Are you a single woman who is trying to attain the "perfect" life but is growing weary of doing everything on her own or waiting on a suitable companion? Are you a married woman with children struggling to take care of the family, appease her spouse, and still maintain her identity? Have you decided to go back to school or pursue a new venture in life but are getting overwhelmed and burned out in the process? Whatever you are struggling with... don't lose hope! Put your trust in the Lord and have faith that he will hear your cry and provide a breakthrough.

Whenever you feel like your faith is fading or that your outlook is becoming jaded, stop and pray! Speak positive affirmations into the atmosphere. Believe and decree that your situation is handled and that you will be a product of greatness! As you renew your faith and hope in the Lord, you will begin to see a shift in your motivation and steadfastness.

JOURNAL: What is it that you are hoping for or seeking from God? In what ways have you become weary? What can you do today to renew your strength? In what ways are you strong?

_____

_____

_____

_____

_____

_____

_____

_____

_____

_____

_____

_____

_____

_____

_____

_____

_____

_____

_____

_____

_____

_____

_____

_____

_____

_____

PRAYER: As you evaluate your strength and weaknesses during your season of waiting, continuously pray and ask God to renew your mind and to help you find encouragement along the way.

PERSONAL REFLECTION:

15

No one can make me feel inferior unless I give them permission to do so.

TIT-FOR-TAT WILL NOT GET YOU THIS-OR-THAT!

"Finally, all of you, be like-minded, be sympathetic, love one another, be compassionate and humble. Do not repay evil with evil or insult with insult. On the contrary, repay evil with blessing, because to this you were called so that you may inherit a blessing." - 1 Peter 3:8-10 NIV

"When they go low, we go high" is a famous catchphrase made popular by former First Lady of the United States, Michelle Obama, at the 2016 Democratic National Convention. She stated this when describing how to handle the "bullies" of the opposing party when Hillary Clinton was running for president. Politics can be a mean game and often brings out the worst in people.

In the recent past, we have witnessed how people can abuse their power and utilize it for wrong. We've also seen how unfair our "justice" system can be. It is unfortunate and hurtful to see these things, especially when trying to live your life as an upstanding citizen; however, we must not repay evil with evil as the Bible has commanded.

What about that person that has wronged you? Trust me, I know it isn't easy to turn the other cheek, hold your tongue, and walk away when you are provoked or when someone is cruel. As strong women, we often want to put the person "in their place" or let them know that we will not let them get away with an insult.

There have been times when I was disrespected, and my intelligence and value were belittled. On many occasions, I was quick to let the person know how I felt and often did so in a combative manner. Honestly, that didn't always go well because it created a heated dialogue. As I have matured, I have learned that there is a way to express your feelings so that it is healthy for you and it gets your point across to the receiver. Our initial response to a difficult encounter should be more sympathetic, and we should want to know why that person is acting the way they are.

The desire to "one-up" someone or participate in tit-for-tat may give us an immediate feeling of gratification; however, in the long run, it puts us on the same level as the person that is acting immature and indecent. It's important to remember that your actions today can affect your blessings tomorrow. What good will it do to continue to argue with someone who will most likely not change their behavior? Is being combative and cunning worth delaying or blocking the blessings you were destined to inherit? As confident women, we know our worth and allow God to handle any insults or injustices for us.

JOURNAL: Are there times when you feel combative, angry, and vengeful? Consider what the root causes of those emotions are? What could you have done differently? What will you do in the future to act more in love?

PRAYER: As you evaluate your wrongs ask God for forgiveness for times when you've mistreated others. Pray that God provides you with the ability to be slow to anger and addresses the root cause of your hurt. Pray that God will also deal accordingly with those who have wronged you.

PERSONAL REFLECTION:

16

I won't live my life in comparison. I am confident in who God has made me.

TRUE BEAUTY COMES FROM WITHIN

"Your beauty should not come from outward adornment, such as elaborate hairstyles and the wearing of gold jewelry or fine clothes. Rather, it should be that of your inner self, the unfading beauty of a gentle and quiet spirit, which is of great worth in God's sight." - 1 Peter 3:3-4 NIV

True beauty lies within. That's a concept that we've heard on more than one occasion; however, society has often shown us differently. For years, a woman's worth has been defined partly by the way she looks, what style of clothes she wears, and other physical attributes. The world likes to draw comparisons of everyday women to those on the television screens or in social media land. Although we are aware that what we see on TV and social media are very often not real, it is hard not to get caught up in the hype of the latest fashion trends, the flawless makeup and hairstyles, and the lavish lifestyles with seemingly perfect relationships to match.

What do we do when we don't fit into those beauty standards or can't maintain such an illusion? What if we cannot afford all of the luxuries or even have a desire to do so? Does that mean that we are not beautiful or worthy of the same respect or admiration? No! As the scripture mentions, it is your inner self that is of great worth. A gentle and quiet spirit is a beauty that never fades. A meek and humble woman, not loud or boisterous, and kind, will always be a standard of beauty that never goes out of style.

"To be beautiful means to accept yourself. You don't need to be accepted by others. You need to accept yourself."- Thich Nhat Hahn

Have you gone through many years of your life not feeling attractive? Maybe you struggle with weight issues or are not happy with your complexion.

Perhaps you've always wanted a particular hairstyle but could not achieve it because of your hair texture. Know that you are uniquely and wonderfully made and that there were no mistakes when God created you! Instead of focusing on everything that you are not, begin to embrace everything that you are! You may find out that your uniqueness is pretty amazing. Please don't believe the heartless individuals in the world that want to force their ideas upon you. Their opinions of you don't matter, and their incognizance does not determine your worth.

JOURNAL: What features or attributes on your body are you happy with? What gifts and talents make you unique? What have you yet to embrace about yourself? Is there any minor thing you can do today that would make you feel beautiful?

_____
_____
_____
_____
_____
_____
_____
_____
_____
_____
_____
_____
_____
_____
_____
_____
_____
_____
_____

PRAYER: Give God all of your insecurities and body issues. Ask God to help you feel more confident and accepting of your appearance. Align yourself with people that love you for who you are, and don't try to change for the sake of others.

PERSONAL REFLECTION:

17

I may not have had the best beginning, but I am determined to have a great finish!

YOU HAVE TO BE EQUIPPED TO ENDURE THE FIGHT

"Finally, be strong in the Lord and in his mighty power. Put on the full armor of God, so that you can take your stand against the devil's schemes. For our struggle is not against flesh and blood, but against the rulers, against the authorities, against the powers of this dark world and against the spiritual forces of evil in the heavenly realms. Therefore put on the full armor of God, so that when the day of evil comes, you may be able to stand your ground, and after you have done everything, to stand." - Ephesians 6:10-13 NIV

Have you ever felt like you were the victim of an unfair fight? Were you attacked when you least expected it? It is one thing to engage in a battle knowingly, but it is another not even to see the battle coming. I've been there before. My day was going smoothly, and then all of a sudden, it seemed like I just walked into a confrontation. I've been in relationships with people where it seemed as if even the smallest problem or argument would turn into World War III just because I expressed a difference of opinion. I felt blinded and disconnected from the individuals, and all I could think of was, "Why did we allow the enemy to win again?"

The Bible warns us that our struggle in this world is not against flesh and blood but against spiritual forces of evil in the heavenly realms. This means that although you think you are fighting with another human being, you actually aren't. You are fighting a force that comes to do nothing else but destroy you. Why? Because the force knows of the power that you hold and the magnificent plans that the Lord has for you.

You will find that you will receive the most attacks when you are happy and attempting to live a life of peace. Don't be surprised that the moment that you declare and decree a change and devote yourself to Christ, that the enemy is listening and planning his next attack.

This is when you will start to see issues with the car breaking down, health failing, your co-workers stressing you out, children running amok, etc.

Despite all of the enemy's schemes, we can stand our ground and be victorious. We just have to be prepared to fight! So, what do we need to be equipped for the fight? Ephesians tells us that we need to put on the full armor of God and wear it at all times. Wearing our battle gear and remaining connected to Christ will assure that we have what we need to overcome any battle. When things get tough, check your inventory and make sure that they are sharpened and ready to be used. You can stand your ground and endure the tests and tricks of the enemy (Ephesians 6: 13-17, NIV).

JOURNAL: Do you feel like you've been fighting in a battle lately? If so, in what ways have you been attacked and you felt weak or powerless? What did you do, or could you have done to persevere?

PRAYER: When you feel overwhelmed and attacked, you need to stop and pray for God's power and strength to endure. Ensure that you have all of the components of the full armor of God at your disposal. Sometimes the tests may be long and frequent, so be patient and long-suffering and never cease to seek God's counsel on how to fight.

PERSONAL REFLECTION:

18

I will lead a life of prosperity!

...NTMENT IN THE WAITING

...know what it is to be in need, and I know what it is to have plenty. I have learned the secret of being content in any and every situation, whether well fed or hungry, whether living in plenty or in want. I can do all this through him who gives me strength." - 4:12-13 NIV

Whether you have made it to the mountain top or you are still in the valley, there is something to be said about your endurance during the journey. Some people have been fortunate enough to have not longed for much. There may have been only a few times when they've had to struggle along their journey. For others, like myself, the journey has been a bit more cumbersome. There have been some highs, lows, and even what felt like the lowest of lows. We've seen a few mountain-tops but also have been in quite a few valleys.

Some people would say that their entire life has been a series of long, drawn-out valleys, and even when they think they have climbed to a peak, they look over and realize that there are many more hills and valleys to go through before reaching the mountain-top.

Regardless of your journey, there can be a reward in how you persevere and make it through. There is beauty in learning, especially when you are being taught a life lesson. Sometimes the lesson is as simple as being patient and content with what you have at the moment.

In life, we will go through seasons. A season to reap and to sow. A season of drought and rain. A season of abundance and a season of lack. Whatever season you're in, know that God is there to protect and guide you and that through Christ, you can do all things! You may stumble through that valley, but with Christ, you can reach new heights of prosperity while still standing. Don't give up! Press on and be confident that your time of victory is coming!

JOURNAL: Analyze the seasons of life that you have recently experienced and evaluate how you fared in each. Were you content while waiting on your change, or were you anxious to move on? What life lessons did you learn in each season? What obstacle do you need Christ's help to overcome?

_____
_____
_____
_____
_____
_____
_____
_____
_____
_____
_____
_____
_____
_____
_____
_____
_____
_____
_____
_____
_____
_____
_____
_____
_____

PRAYER: Pray that the Lord will provide you with patience and strength when you are weak and when you feel like giving in. Try to find the lesson in each season of your life so that it will become the wisdom that you need to make it through similar seasons in the future.

PERSONAL REFLECTION:

19

I am a child of God. I am worthy, and I deserve the best.

HOPE FOR WIDOWS AND THOSE WITHOUT FATHERS

"A father to the fatherless, a defender of widows, is God in his holy dwelling." - Psalm 68: 5 NIV

Did you grow up in a home where your father was not around, and you experienced a yearning for a love you never knew? You may have had trouble understanding why he wasn't around and questioned if you'd done something to keep him away. You may have experienced feelings of abandonment, rejection, and insecurities, especially if your father has passed away. Girls who grow up without fathers in the household often struggle with low self-esteem or feeling unworthy. Many times, their view on how they should be treated or loved by a man is altered. That altered view can lead to seeking attention and love in all the wrong places.

What happens when a woman becomes a widow? Does she feel any less abandoned or less confident in who she is? No, she often feels just as lost, uncertain, unworthy, and possibly even rejected by God. Widows not only have to deal with grieving the love of their life, but they also feel that they have to appear to be strong for the rest of the family. They often question whether or not they can make it without their spouse or if they will ever be able to love in that way again.

Whether you are dealing with daddy issues or have lost your spouse, know that all is not lost, and there is still hope. You can be the strong, confident, brave, and beloved woman that God has called you to be regardless. Rest assured that you have a father in Heaven who is greater than any man on this earth. If you feel unloved, remember that Christ showed his ultimate love for you by sacrificing His life on the cross. Every good thing that you have or have ever had has been a blessing from God because of His love and mercies toward you.

When you feel unvalued or unseen, remember that Christ is always with you. His holy spirit is there to comfort you. You are so valuable to Him that He works on your behalf daily, even when you don't even value yourself. You're a child of God and a part of a royal lineage.

You have so much potential to excel despite the open wound you may have from your earthly father being absent. Never feel that you have to downgrade your self-respect or worth to be loved by a man.

When you feel unsure about the future, trust that God will not only make a way of provision for you but that He will be your protector, your guide, and your resource. Trust that God's plan and will for your life are perfect and that you were never forgotten or rejected by Him.

JOURNAL: Have you experienced any daddy issues, or a loss of a spouse or father figure in your life? If so, in what ways has that affected you? In what ways have you demonstrated that God is your Father and your source of direction and comfort?

....
....
....
....
....
....
....
....
....
....
....
....
....
....
....
....
....
....
....
....

PRAYER: If you are struggling, ask God to protect, lead, and comfort you as a father or a spouse would. Cleave to Him as a child and cast all of your cares upon Him because He loves you.

PERSONAL REFLECTION:

My family and I are happy, healthy, and blessed.

MEDICINE FOR OUR SOULS

"A cheerful heart is good medicine, but a crushed spirit dries up the bones." - Proverbs 17:22 NIV

There is a connection between our mood and physical health. You probably know or have heard of someone who is always positive and in an upbeat mood even when not feeling well. Or maybe even an elderly person who is still vibrant, full of life, and healthy overall. I often think of one of my dear cousins who passed away in her early 30's from kidney failure. Every time I saw her, she had a smile on her face and appeared to be in good spirits despite her grim prognosis and the painful bouts of dialysis. I believe that it was her attitude and will to press on, in addition to God's mercy, that allowed her to live as long as she did.

Have you ever been sad or depressed, and you can physically feel the weight of the sadness? Like a disease, emotional pain can also affect your physical abilities. I've experienced times when the heaviness from stress impeded my ability to get out of bed or off the couch. Has your broken heart caused you to start experiencing other ailments like depression, fatigue, rapid weight gain/loss, etc.? It's time to bring some happiness back into your life! As Proverbs alluded, your attitude and spirit have the power to either bring healing or continued sickness.

What can you do to change your mood and promote healing? Focus on the good things that have happened to you or things you are thankful for. Everyone has something to be grateful for. Don't focus on what you cannot change or control at the moment regarding your tough situation. You will need to pray and give that burden to The Lord. Next, get up! I know it may not be easy, but you can do it! Part of the fight is just getting up and out of the muck we are stuck in.

Consider also calling a friend, or a loved one, that you know will either provide you with good conversation, a laugh, or both. When possible, surround yourself with others. There have been many times when I did not want to meet with a friend or attend a workout class, but once I did, I felt so much better than I did before. Remember, healing starts within, and as we build confidence, we also have to allow some healing to occur in areas where we have felt broken.

JOURNAL: Reflect on how your mood has affected you physically and mentally? Do you see any areas of change needed? Where are you shrinking back in life because you simply don't feel well? What makes you happy?

....
....
....
....
....
....
....
....
....
....
....
....
....
....
....
....
....
....
....
....
....
....
....
....
....
....
....

PRAYER: Determine what triggers cause your mood to fluctuate and pray specifically for healing in those areas. Pray for increased happiness and a cheerful spirit.

PERSONAL REFLECTION:

21

I will use the gifts and talents that God has given me to be a blessing to others.

COMFORT FOR THOSE WHO COMFORT OTHERS

"Praise be to the God and Father of our Lord Jesus Christ, the Father of compassion and the God of all comfort, 4 who comforts us in all our troubles, so that we can comfort those in any trouble with the comfort we ourselves receive from God." – II Corinthians 1:3-4 NIV

It is often said that you can't pour from an empty cup. Crops need water and sunlight to grow to eventually become a source of nourishment. Even our vehicles have to be refueled in order to provide us with transportation to get from here and there. This may come as a shock, but even you -- the superwoman caretaker extraordinaire -- need to be comforted and re-energized to continue to be there for and support others. You're human. At some point, your cup will "runneth" low. Hardships and trouble will come. Your patience will be tested, and your confidence in your abilities will dissipate. Who is there to comfort those that feel like they have no shoulder to lean on? Who will be there to swoop in and save the day for us when we feel so defeated and broken? Who will be there to lift our esteem when we feel unconfident in the work we are doing?

As a mother, a single mother at that, I know how it feels just to want a little help. To just want someone else to make all the rounds, help with school, make sure the child is fed, happy, and disciplined when needed. You may have the immense responsibility of taking care of an elderly parent or handicapped loved one and, at times, may not feel that you are always the most capable one to make all of the right decisions. You may be a leader in the church or a counselor who is constantly motivating and encouraging others but rarely have anyone to do the same for you. Maybe you are the only one in your household that can locate resources for your family, and you've got to be that strong advocate even when you don't know how.

Regardless of your situation, know that God is with you! Take confidence in knowing that there is someone mightier than you and available to help you. He is your strength. He has all the answers. When your heart is broken and the tears are flowing, know that Christ will dry every tear and mend every broken heart. He is the Great Comforter. His Holy Spirit is there to shower us with love and provide the embrace we are yearning for. When you feel overwhelmed, don't give up. Know that just as you provide comfort to others, He will do the same for you!

JOURNAL: What are the areas of your life where you feel that you need the most support? What types of resources or support are available to you now? What could be done to make your daily load a bit easier? What self-care can you begin to practice on a routine basis?

PRAYER: When you just need to feel comforted and loved, pray that the Holy Spirit will embrace you when you need it most. Ask God to send you resources and help to make your responsibilities a little less difficult to manage. Be willing to accept the help when a reasonable solution is presented.

PERSONAL REFLECTION:

22

I will not let shame make me walk with my head held down.

WHEN TROUBLE TRIED TO DEVOUR ME

"Who shall separate us from the love of Christ? Shall trouble or hardship or persecution or famine or nakedness or danger or sword? 36 As it is written: "For your sake we face death all day long; we are considered as sheep to be slaughtered." 37 No, in all these things we are more than conquerors through him who loved us."
- Romans 8:35- 37 NIV

We were created to handle difficult things. We were designed with the proper anatomy to handle the harsh conditions of the environment and weather the storms of life. When pains like heartbreak, disappointment, and cruelty pierce us, we have the innate ability to heal those wounds.

If you've lived on this earth long enough, you will have experienced some sort of hardship or persecution from others. Even children have to share the journey of learning how to navigate through difficult situations on their own.

As with children, there is a point at which we must look to someone that we trust for assistance, love, and guidance. As children of God, we are like his sheep, and He is our shepherd. Although we face persecution, intimidating scenes, and near-death situations daily, God is there to protect us and save us from being consumed.

It was terrible what happened to me, but I am not a terrible person.
It hurt so bad, but I don't have to live in agony.

Some things that you may have experienced in life may have broken your spirit immensely. If you've been broken down physically or mentally, you don't have to live like a victim or wear a scarlet letter across your chest. Trauma and abuse have not made you useless or weak. Lack and neglect may have been present at one point in time, but you are not a castaway; you have a purpose. Not only is God a forgiving God he can also wipe your slate clean. It doesn't matter how low, exposed, or naked you feel, Christ is a redeemer, and He loves us regardless!

Guilt and shame tend to make us feel inferior so much that even when we've been forgiven or delivered, we still don't feel worthy. Surviving difficulties and trouble can take such a toll on us that we may feel a little disjointed once we make it to the other side. As we work on our healing, know that God will be with us every step of the way. Don't feel ashamed to talk to Him about your problems or pray about the same things repeatedly. It may take all of that to restore wholeness. Let nothing separate you from Christ and His desire to have an intimate relationship with you.

JOURNAL: Reflect on how you have overcome troubling situations in the past. How did you handle them, and what could you have done differently to better handle them? Are there obstacles or fears in your life that you are still facing? What can you do to ensure that you will not allow negative experiences to affect your relationship with Christ or your outlook on a positive future?

PRAYER: Pray for guidance to get through the difficult times, strength, and a renovated mind to begin to heal your physical and emotional wounds and for comfort along the way. If you feel guilty or shameful about anything in your past, ask God to forgive you and wipe your slate clean so that you can begin living a guilt-free and optimistic lifestyle.

PERSONAL REFLECTION:

23

I am loved by the greatest, and I'm capable of showing love to others.

HOPE FOR THOSE WHO HAVE NOT BEEN LOVED THE RIGHT WAY

"Love is patient, love is kind. It does not envy, it does not boast, it is not proud. It does not dishonor others, it is not self-seeking, it is not easily angered, it keeps no record of wrongs. Love does not delight in evil but rejoices with the truth. 7 It always protects, always trusts, always hopes, always perseveres."
- I Corinthians 13:4-7 NIV

Have you ever wondered how someone could say I love you when you depart them, and then you don't hear from them for months at a time, not even to check in to see if you are okay? What about when that friend or family member tells you that they love you, but then you later hear that they are talking about you behind your back, or they expect you to help them in a time of need, but they are hardly ever able to help you out when you need it? One of the more puzzling examples is when you are in a relationship with someone, regardless of how juvenile it may be, and they say they love you but still do things to upset or harm you.

The type of love defined in I Corinthians above is called Agape love. This is the selfless, unconditional love that the Bible talks about. Have you ever experienced it? Most have likely experienced it in bits and pieces but not as a whole. Maybe you weren't even aware that this was even a type of love at all and therefore have never allowed yourself to love someone in this fashion.

What happens when you become an adult and realize that you've never been loved the Agape way? Maybe you weren't raised this way. It is possible that your parents or guardians did not know how or weren't aware of how to show this kind of love. A presence of abuse in the household can also lead to family members not even knowing what proper love and affection are. Sometimes we expect people to give us a level of admiration and respect that they just aren't capable of giving us.

Sis, I know how difficult it is to be in love with someone who is not returning the same love to you. I have heard all of the rumblings of the "L-word," but when I took the time to dissect the Bible's definition of love, I realized that several things were missing.

It seemed as if the person I loved dearly was frequently angry with me, kept records of wrongdoings, didn't protect me, and did not persevere the relationship when the going got tough. It baffled me that this person could adamantly express love for me vocally but showed it contrarily. Because of this, I began to think that something was wrong with me; I wasn't capable of being loved in the Agape way or simply was unworthy of the need that I felt. It crushed my spirit because I didn't get enough of it when I was a little girl and was growing tired of not finding it as an adult.

If you have been in similar situations, know that God is love personified. If we are ever in need of a love refill, who's greater than God to provide it? Regardless of who didn't provide you with the love you needed, know that you still deserve it. One person's inability to love you the right way is not a measure of your value and does not signal your ability to show someone else true Godly love.

If you are not in a relationship that is serving you, whether it be family, friend, or loved one, acknowledge that you deserve more. Communicate to that person what you need to fill your love tank appropriately and listen for their needs as well. Pursue relationships that are fulfilling to the path you seek in life, and remember that someone out there will love you for who you are!

JOURNAL: Reflect on times in your life when you have been shown Agape love and when you may have given it to others. How did it feel? Have there been relationships in your life where you were not loved the right way? How did that affect you? What steps can you take to improve the quality of relationships in your life?

_____

_____

_____

_____

_____

_____

_____

_____

_____

PRAYER: If you've experienced shortcomings in receiving the love and attention that you needed from someone important to you, pray and ask God to heal your heart from that hurt. Pray that you will not only learn how to love others in the Agape way but that you will also learn to love yourself more than ever before. When feeling unvalued or loved, cleave to God and His Word as reminders of how much He cares for you.

PERSONAL REFLECTION:

_____

_____

_____

_____

_____

_____

_____

_____

_____

_____

_____

_____

_____

_____

_____

_____

24

It is already done! I believe it and claim it!

BELIEVING THAT IT WILL ALL WORK OUT

"And we know that in all things God works for the good of those who love him, who] have been called according to his purpose." - Romans 8:28 NIV

It's funny how a rainbow is formed. When it rains and gets dark during the day, the sunlight still wants to peek through. When the sunlight peers through the raindrops at just the right angle, light in the form of several colors begins to reflect. Usually, when we can see the rainbow, we know that the storm or rain is over. Soon after, we can start to expect the darkness to fade away and the sunlight to shine bright again. The rainbow is a pleasant sign that the storm is over, and everything will go back to normal. We believe this because experience and science have shown us that this is true.

The same is true for our belief in God when it comes to working things out for us. The Bible tells us that All Things will work for the good of those who love Him. Experience, even when we try to ignore it, will also prove to us that God will work out our every concern. Think back to that time when God spared your life from the car accident that could've been fatal or how He allowed you to make it through one of the largest ordeals of our lifetimes, the COVID-19 pandemic. Sometimes our situations can be so cloudy and dark that we allow our mind to focus on the current outlook while neglecting what we know to be true...that he will work everything out for us in the end.

Romans 8 reminds us that in ALL things, God works for the good. This means that no matter how horrible or complicated the issue is, it can and will work out for good. Sometimes we forget to take even our smallest concerns to God and try to handle them on our own. Often, we fail or become overwhelmed with trying to tackle them by ourselves. Again, we must remember that ALL things does not have a limit to size or quantity. It means every single thing, every single time.

So, why does this hold true? How can we be reassured that the mountain that we are staring at will be moved? The answer is because Christ does not fail! We are called to receive his blessings and His will for our lives. All we have to do is love and believe Him. Believing is actually one of the simplest things that we can do.

Walking confidently is consistent with having faith and believing that while we may not have it all together and may have some problems that need to be resolved, we can walk tall and be assured that our God will work everything out!

JOURNAL: Compare your recent years to the concept of the rainbow. In what ways did God bring you out of a gloomy situation and into the emergence of sunshine? Like the rainbow, were you given any signs along the way that things would work out?

....
....
....
....
....
....
....
....
....
....
....
....
....
....
....
....
....
....
....
....

PRAYER: Give thanks to God for the good things that have happened in your life and the rainbows he's allowed you to see. Pray that you will continue to have faith that He will stay by your side and will allow everything to work out despite how bad it looks. Be sure to tell Him often that you love Him and appreciate all of His mercies towards you.

PERSONAL REFLECTION:

25

I exude confidence, faith, and prosperity!

MAN'S PRIZED POSSESSION: A GOOD WOMAN

"He who finds a wife finds what is good and receives favor from the Lord." - Proverbs 18:22 NIV

You've heard it before, the all too common sayings: *"Happy Wife, Happy Life!"* and "Behind every great man is a great wife." Commonly used and assumed, surprisingly, there are so many good women out there who are still single, looking for a life partner, and wondering if they will ever become a wife. They've done all of the things to make themselves a good catch...obtained an education, established a career, taken on leadership roles, and became bosses in their own ways. Beautiful inside and out, strong and determined, but have not yet been able to call themselves a wife or secure the long-term marriage that they'd hoped for. Remember that there is a time and a season for everything, and that patience is a virtue.

To everything, there is a season and a time to every purpose under the heaven.
- (King James Version, Holy Bible. Ecclesiastes 3:1)

If you feel like you've done everything right to make yourself a good catch, but you still haven't found Mr. Right, don't lose hope! There is someone out there for you that will check off the majority of those items on your checklist and make you happy. Don't settle for Mr. Right Now just because you are lonely or impatient. You have so much to offer the right person. Even if you have made mistakes in the past, the changes you have made to improve should not be wasted on a person who doesn't deserve to reap the benefits.

If you are in a relationship with a man who has not realized the gem he has in front of him, remind him that you are a good woman and worthy of becoming a wife. As the scripture states, He who finds a wife finds something good, and he will receive favor from the Lord. I don't know about you, but I wouldn't want to delay my favor and blessings because I was unsure or not ready to commit to something beautiful.

Know your worth, Sis, and know when it's time to move on. Staying with someone that hasn't realized that his prized possession is right in his face is unproductive.

You may be in a waiting season, and that is okay. Take this time to continue to make yourself the best woman that you can be. Enjoy doing things that make you happy and achieve your goals. Don't fall into the notion that just because you are single that something is wrong with you. That is simply a lie from the enemy. You are a gem and a prized possession for whomever God sees fit to place in your life.

JOURNAL: Reflect on what makes you a "good catch." What do you love about yourself and want to share with others? What qualities are you seeking in a husband if unmarried? If married, are you and your husband meeting each other's expectations?

PRAYER: If you are still looking to become a wife, ask God to send the right spouse into your life and for the ability to recognize him when you see him. In the meantime, pray that God will allow you to be patient and content with "doing you" and accomplishing your own dreams. If you are married, pray that you will continue to be a great spouse and blessing to your husband while still being able to do things that make you happy and fulfilled in life as well.

PERSONAL REFLECTION:

The Confidence Building Tool

This tool is designed to aid you in building confidence in the areas of your life where you may feel like you are lacking. Release your insecurities from your head and write them down on paper. Develop an achievable action plan, meditate on it, and document your progress along the way.

What area of my life could use a boost of confidence?

What can I do "now" to increase confidence in those areas?

Things I Love About Myself

Favorite Confidence Quotes

How will I hold myself accountable?

Made in the USA
Monee, IL
27 October 2022

16646037R20063